'Shareen K. Murayama weaves tog
is ode and elegy in this beautiful, r
"Every minute, every year, you iceb......., one writes, referencing a
seemingly-ceaseless grief, one that is rooted in the present and a
product of inherited trauma. Indeed, this collection investigates
the personal and collective losses: of a mother, of a relationship,
of a language, of a species, and of people of color—and, more
specifically, fellow Asian Americans—who have been victims of
white violence. Balancing personal details with allusions to folklore,
visual art, and film, these poems insist on bearing witness. "I hate
when people say moving on," Murayama writes, and this collection
eschews moving on—serving instead as a catalog of remembrances,
a refusal to forget.'

Despy Boutris, *Burials* (Bull City Press, 2022) and Editor-in-Chief
of *The West Review*

'This stunning collection weaves scent, sight and sound into a
tapestry—one that would be a waste mounted to a wall and allowed
to collect dust. These poems should be wrapped around weary
shoulders, used as a barrier against frigid realities. The poems
within *Housebreak* overflow with distance and grief, but Shareen
Murayama proves herself a sure navigator in a sea of sadness. When
she wrote the line, "I wield the heart commanding / your attention"
she couldn't have known just how right those words were, how their
truth would echo far beyond the poem of their origin.'

Raphael Jenkins, 2022 Periplus Fellow and Poetry Editor,
Passengers Press

'In this astonishing collection, Shareen Murayama tenderly navigates the wild intimacy of grief. *Housebreak* speaks to grief that is both deeply personal and shared, from the loss of loved ones to communal and national wounds. Traversing a landscape that includes a mother's dementia and a zombie apocalypse, this work is sure to surprise you as much as it will move you. Murayama writes, "We strive to live in the pocket of the wave where the energy is brightest." So too, these poems, while haunted by profound loss, careen ceaselessly toward light'.

Erin Mizrahi, Editor-in-Chief *Cobra Milk Journal*

HOUSEBREAK

Shareen K. Murayama is the author of the poetry chapbook *Hey Girl, Are You in the Experimental Group?* (Small Harbor Publishing, 2022). She is a Japanese American, Okinawan American poet and educator. She's a 2021 Best Microfiction winner, a poetry reader for *The Adroit Journal*, and Assistant CNF Editor for *JMWW*. Her works have been published or forthcoming in *The McNeese Review*, *The Willowherb Review*, *National Flash Fiction*, *The Margins*, *Bamboo Ridge Press*, and elsewhere. She lives in Honolulu, Hawai'i. You can find her on IG and Twitter @ambusypoeming.

Housebreak

Published by Bad Betty Press in 2022
www.badbettypress.com

Cover design by Amy Acre
Photography courtesy of Domenico Paolella

Printed and bound in the United Kingdom

A CIP record of this book is available from the British Library.

ISBN: 978-1-913268-30-5

Supported using public funding by

ARTS COUNCIL ENGLAND

LOTTERY FUNDED

Housebreak

BAD BETTY PRESS

Housebreak

* with gratitude for my ohana
the ones beneath the sun
the ones beyond the stars

Contents

Body Language

It starts in the middle, what fills us—or in the
long nerve of the thigh. *Felt like a giant thumb,
pushing down on my back*, she said. We lined
mushrooms and carrots, rolled rice into sushi. I
wasn't prepared to eat all I'd make ugly. A year
on her knees, quilted with psalm. Her body
rocks forward. *why*. She falls back
into the present. We fashioned white beds on
green seaweed, a story with holes. God had
fixed her back so she could stand. I connect the
dots: *son's*. *death*. She doesn't know English
for *breakdown*. My window frames the moon,
another tale with no body. I roll over the edge,
crimp softly in showers. I ferry more words
than my grandmother, yet pray for definitions:
citizen. *home*. There's a madness running in
ovals when executive threats are the spine of
this country. Everything that's ugly, I want to
root out. But I have faith in folktales, like my
grandmother's story. Anyone could be saved or
eaten. Their tongues cut out.

Salt as Preservative

I was thinking about yo momma jokes—
how we entertain the ridiculous

took a picture of her last Christmas, still printing
how we're tickled by alternate universes

takes an hour for her to cook minute rice
doesn't listen to her doctors.

Half of the time, I've become
half of my mother.

We're recipients of drop-dead
(not gorgeous) genes

being first-in-the-family garners
irregular distance from others.

When I cry tears of laughter
it's really a heart-felt attempt

to draw out excessive water
create less conducive grounds

for germs—predisposed & self-inflicted—
a method for curing meat.

Birthmark

I hold cards worth the most points closest to my chest:

black pines with tickling hairs   yellow tips capped

      a crane stands on one foot
      red-crested head looks back   on the red
sun as a child

      I overlooked   moons.peonies I chase

cards bearing animals   as an adult
as a burnt orange boar
in bush.clover

the deer's head & the autumn leaves
turn in time

Each animal in my hand
wet in solitude:
      orange & red   chrysanthemums   bloom a man

an umbrella comes across   a frog

while talons full-scoop   spindly flowers
                                          blood red like
                                          a phoenix.my mother

I was fuller than a picture. almost straight. are irises.   purple hearts.
                                                                   rounded.

their star-shaped season. leaves

your hand empty again
You are not versed in how to read what's already left.

S-shaped necks. Kowtow low. Then flap—

            wings.dance

a bush warbler on plum blossoms
faces west   prepares to sing

a story on a card.   you refuse

to play

You're Trapped in School, and Your Classmates Are Turning into Zombies

This is not a drill.
This is a supplemental college essay prompt. It's
Inbound. Seek.

The five items you'd bring and where you'd hide?

1. My mom because she parades extra opinions.
But she's dead now. Not zombie dead.
2. My lunch bag because now is all we can count.
3. A master key with no knowledge, no respite from bodily harm.
It's probably in the pocket of the dead with broom in
hand. She'd bake mooncakes for teachers
who knew her name. I never got mooncakes. I confess. Sometimes
I can be an asshole.

Silence.
She's getting closer, Hawai'i.
EMERGENCY ALERT.

4. A book, a bible. A weapon. No, no.
4. Rumi's poem: *We are going to sky. Who wants to come with us?*
No one moves, but fingers swipe.
4. A joke. Shelter on an island 43 miles wide.
4. First aid supplies. But there's no kit for wounds that size.
4. A short wave radio that's hidden in my backpack of
knives and an axe that I take daily to school. I confess:

There's no defense for a ballistic missile.
4. Forgiveness in a bottle that I could filter blame, regret, absolution
for assholes.
It's the heaviest item to lug—leave it behind.

Where would I hide?
In plain sight of all the flowers on the island,
swaying in the trade winds,
moving and not moving together.
We have nowhere to go.
And your fifth item?

5. A prayer for a mossy acceptance.

Defect

For the Asian Americans who did not become doctors

From time to time, my mother calls and asks how I am doing. It's May, closing of grades, another year, and the same. The mountain doves posture their bird-brains, planting nests in frangible locations. It rains patches of hay that I don't fish from the lawn and gutters. My mother sends news to me from our family—the ones that don't speak of me *(ill or well)* because no one flocks to me in an emergency. Her silence imitates them. I look over my valley, a quiet community of those not recognized within or without. In recent years, whole family units have defected here, the Land of Pish, denuded of old wives' tales. At customs, suitcases are screened for antiquated hooks and sinkers, while hope chests are recycled for the mountain doves. Everyone feels so much lighter and pink. My mother calls from time to time, from some other distant land, and asks how I am doing, and tells me *your shoes have always held more water than mine.* Sometimes we don't talk. We allow the birds to sing, before and after nesting, to anyone and no one.

Reservations as Future Tense

A nut can be seen as either a seed or a fruit. Six months from now,
my sister will voluntarily check herself into a mental health facility.

To brush against people on this side of the glass and whisper, wonder.
What is your relationship to the patient?

My sister will laugh over the phone and say, *There are crazy people here.*
Her roommate will announce that she's Satan, and give her a copy

of the New Testament. She'll comment how restricting: visiting hours,
bottled drinks, short telephone cords.

Is it like *One Flew Over the Cuckoo's Nest* or *Girl, Interrupted?*
I'll ask. She'll say she hasn't seen those movies.

On the anniversary of Anthony Bourdain's dying, my sister
will choose not to. *More eyes watching me, checking on me.*

I'll wish I had more eyes for her. I can tell her about the warmth
of the ebb-tide for those who agree to a voluntary hold.

But I will never lie to my sister.

Housebreak

I know diablo means *devil* & anthos means *flower*
what you want me to spread—
illegal entries skirt folds of the land
                             It's summer & I wait for fidelity to bloom
                             A stonewall, blue gravel, an off ramp to take
                             I call attention to everything but you

You say *tongue* & *peninsula*; I think babydoll
& betrayal, what I long for weekend-ly
I breathe in, count backwards from you
                             They say to check on your loved ones
                             but there are worse symbols I could inflict:
                             what I learned from my mother
My father's face is a sidewalk
peppered with flyers
A pocket empty of coins & sounds
                             My face as placeholder for sporting events
                             Coffee stains on a coffee table
                             Never have I thrown a fight
My father's face lines mine over time
the warmth of your arm, the sag of a roof
I wonder if they can be saved?
                             At the start of relationships
                             I vacillate if I can pass
                             on love—
when loyalty spins too domestic
I imagine its blades—
our initials notched on bamboo
                             insert only the parts of me
                             I can sacrifice

Forecast

After Traci Brimhall

We monitor the mid-tides casting mist
of equal height, shattered pearls frosted
on lips. You uncoil the garden hose,
water blue ginger, the shisho,
and nasubi—a meal and accessories
for a hipster bistro. *It's all overpriced,*
you tell me after a Sunday brunch
when the light of our day-date recedes.
The shine of our new, settles, like me.
Disappointed, you say: *It's for the ambience,*
as if wooden benches and waterfalls
aren't nestlike, future-tense fixtures.
I'm melancholy when you recall time with your ex's
husky in parks, on road trips. One would think
you cared more for the animal than your wife.
For years, you vacuumed traces of hair after they'd left.
I want the steady of companionship. A tying.
Every day we scan the ocean, avoid surfing at low tide,
the sharp reef protrudes, glistening like a bed of knives.

tues morn

i threw a big dinner party
w chicken bones on
plates in the sink leftovers.
i slept w a girl w short hair
who loaned me her art
for tues wed n thursday.
but i didnt see thm.
i was trying to explain,
whn the sound of wheels
of my husband's suitcase rolled
down the hallway.
i wanted to hide the beautiful
girl w short hair

On Using My Bones to Make Your Bread

You wake to find life is filtered coffee grounds
spilled between ever and after

When the evening's lullaby enchants no more
and the breadcrumbs in your bedsheets
are really breadcrumbs in your bedsheets

The morning after disrobing yourself
of broken fairytales, you run screaming
and yanking at faded silk ribbons
hanging from every room in your house

What We Do When We Run Out of Elephants

Today the volume button on my phone
stopped working.
No. I should say *died*.
I hate saying *died*.
Your voicemails cradled metallic;
my pockets too thin.

They say a hundred elephants are killed each day:
a living room toothless times a hundred.
They say elephants bury their dead.
Tympanic shrills and gentle nudging
shaking against what is passing: tentacular.
A limbic silence wakes the community
tossing branches and leaves on the not moving.
Members of the herd will stay with the body for days
before moving on.
I hate when people say *moving on*.

Today the volume button on my phone died.
What will we do when what powers us
stops moving—
a gentle nudge, shaking against
what's already moved on.

Exploded as in Fairy Tale

At the corner of Warren and 4th, I stood in front of a church
  congenital as in existing at or before birth

Where the grassy lawn puckered at the chain-linked fence
  as in certain mental/physical traits which may be hereditary

I overheard a young woman say into her phone, *We're going to be fine.*
  as in not to be confused with genitalia or congenial

She said, *Things are falling into place.*
  as in improper development
I'm still angry with God for taking you away
  as in things are falling (still) into place:

> eggshells & sunlight
> bright orange humps of flames
> a mouth pressed together

She said, *Life is good.* Longer pause. *Yeah, all the acronyms.*
  Only 13 points in Scrabble

I walk away from slips of white paper and a tin box for prayers
  as in structural defect of the heart

A Hundred-Pound Test Line

In every game, there's at least one loser. Dementia erases small dinners with friends, three a.m. bottles of wine. By three p.m., Mom retained her shape and told you: *You don't know anything about love.*

I wonder how long a line with no memory stays straight. Your silence created less friction, which enabled longer, smoother casts. Like how a week-old bruise is also wine and cognac. One time it was a car crash we survived: *I don't want you to want me anymore*, she said.

You pinned a photo of a blue marlin, your biggest catch, above a shelf holding books about sharks and wines, lures and other types of tackle. When I felt bravest, I would open one of your books to revisit the hole in a man, where a thigh might connect to a hip or groin. The victim of an 18-foot tiger shark attack on a gurney. Why do hands wrapped around a leg mean something has already left us?

When you claimed you had to travel for work, I understood how a body could be there and not. Later, I feared angrier attacks that left invisible scars, like locusts. A thousand thousand legs fluttering, materializing: a recurring motif in our dining room.

For decades, the locusts would morph, growing physically stronger, their bodies turning darker. Each week a different story, the same line—or maybe a cross—her demarcation against infidelity. Subjecting yourself to ridicule never stopped the wrath until after you died. When your body was no longer there and not remembered straightly, then she would say: *He really did take care of me.* Sometimes less memory is better.

to *deadhead* plants means to remove their spent flowers

After Hala Alyan

My brain is 80 percent water
I love how it nibbles the skin

        [inside out]

*

My grandmother housed sun-faded curtains of no particular color.
She said *never marry* as we ate creamed crackers. In my dreams,
her skin is almost white. I throw out the window. My-mom-as-a-
young-girl climbs out the window, fleeing to a crematorium.

*

        [skirting the folds of the new]

I allow men and bodysurfing to push me into new spaces. A spray is
also love at funerals.
Floating in my mother's womb, I recall

*

when I love the ocean is
when I love the wrong woman

        [sans a life worth lying about]

*

There's never a shortage of water or knives. The body folds inward like yesterday's paper. I once saw three stingrays stirring the bay's blackness. A ripple, sometimes, is the only evidence of life.

*

My-mom-as-a-young-girl dreamt fires were licking her body. There's always a shortage of water. I kicked my windshield out, tonguing the word *wrong*. I couldn't learn to love something that someone else once loved. I lied to myself. My brain is mostly water. I'll never forget a group of stingrays is called a

[fever]

The Blue Circus

After the painting of the same name by Marc Chagall

How stained and cyan'd is one's childhood   when

      anticipation meets the wildest   I wield the heart   commanding

      your attention   my green   my horse and I   revel

under the gold sky   coined   a crescent moon for

      change my fault   leaning into a fall

      a blue fish sends flowers for her   arrival of the heart

tattoos trail   the sides of her pink

are the last   to touch   the sandy arena

Winds Are Named for the Direction They Are Heading

Offshore winds funnel down the mountain
    four cities on fire are grazed; it
        bottom-turns left through her Hannah Montana blanket,
kissing her seven-year-old head goodnight.
    Always and never the officer—discharged, fired.
        This new-to-me wind cliffs through my backpack,
the leaf of paper I pen on: "careless discharge of weapon"
    say *killed*
        say *murdered*
Shearing a family rust-stained and winded: "causing death"
    say *girl-slaughter*
        say *Aiyana's murderer*
She would have graduated from high school this year.
    The offshore winds tear into the mourning,
        lanterning streets, five stop signs ignored
say *law*   *less*
        "He's on vacation."
    The offshore winds skip over the broken people
toward the last break, where it slaps and slows water,
    creates a well-formed wave
        with a wall full meaty to carve through,
inflicting the perfect conditions.

Irreverent Y

On the occasion of my partner Craig's autopsy

They cut you from each shoulder joint
to the middle of your chest
where my head would vibrate
to your deep, deep voice:

> a sighing of a hundred bees
> beneath a white cotton sheet

Fractured Planes: An Empty Defense Mechanism

It's the spaces between vertebrae that allow lizards to drop their tail
I was watching this thing you just said hanging in the air between
us:

Papa's in the sky? Can we drive to him?
My skin and muscles, blood and nerves, separate—

an amputation that affects my sense of balance
like one-way texts and much too much listening on your side

The reproductive process stops and
bundles of muscle fold over exposed bone

They say the end will dry into a cap
My skin grows over a silence slit long

ways sunflower petals roll over the crest
ways I bump into another form of myself:

dried pistils and stamens, yellow curves, dotted lines—
a flower stretched over a hundred yards

When it grows back, the tail's not the same length or color
and can't be dropped again until you nod and tell me, *Papa's at home.*

He's just home now.

Elasticity

Half of me wants to perch on the church's patina and press
flowers, dry beauty is all make-believe dogma.

I've once held the word god its spindle-shape is
tapered at both ends. Today I feel like the blue sky

divided by blue ocean like how my mother and I are horses
on a Chinese calendar; we are two-dimensional women

to bet on, women at war only one of us falling
failing to feel betrayal. At times I reel in self-acceptance.

My foraging location is the space between the eyes and nostrils
of a snake. Some call it a *lore.* I want to communicate my ownership

of a leaf making them less dangerous. I know it's keeping me
safer from others, which hardens the skin.

Like gravity and the sun, we get burned loving what we love.

Hā means breath in Hawaiian

1. In ancient Hawai'i, it was important to exchange breath—to smell the living—when greeting someone. *Alo* means presence, front, or face. Combined it can be summed up as the presence of (Divine) Breath. *Aloha.*

2. The Hawaiian word for wind is *makani*, but there are as many names as the Inuit have for snow. Some winds were named according to their geographic locations: 'Alahonua (Hilo), Apa'apa'a (Kohala, Hawai'i), Alahou (Moloka'i), Kaua'ula (Lahaina), and 'Ahiu (Kahana, O'ahu).

3. If the winds borrowed names of places, then how shall we name a sigh? As originating in the thorax or trachea or long-term longing?

4. Ancient Hawaiians would greet one another by touching each other's nose bridges and inhaling the hā (the breath of life) and mana (the spiritual power between two people).

5. In an interview, Maggie Nelson was asked what she made of the "leaning against" of other texts in her work. She posits that it's not a leaning against others, but our consciousnesses deeply intertwined, like "a thick soul-and-mind soup."

6. And if all of us make up a collective consciousness of thoughts, poems, and art, then what of those floating thoughts from our ancestors before us? And before them? Does the rope unravel because one thread dies? Are we drifting around the world as we inhale and recycle mana?

7. I told my partner I was thinking of writing a collection on the mysteriousness of winds, he looked flummoxed and asked, "As in 'can of beans'?"

8. When Thich Nhat Hanh says the river we bathe in today is the same river we bathed in yesterday, is everyone as intimate with grief?

9. Can I tell my 17-year old niece, *She is the same mother you always had, but different now that she's dead*? Yesterday's loss is still today's river to cross.

10. The best kind of wind comes once a year when blowing out birthday candles. It's said that the ritual promises magical and mythical powers–except for those over fourteen and under one hundred.

11. Half a year after my sister-in-law's death, her daughter confides in me: "I'm starting to understand now. Not only was she not there for my high school graduation, but she won't be there for my next one, nor for my sister's, nor my wedding. And if I have kids, they won't have a grandmother." I hug her hard and try not to think of my mom sitting in the care home with only the TV watching her.

12. I don't take to the verb *wind*, like *whine*. *I will wind up, crank up, increase the tension until your panties twist and eyeballs pop out of your nerves* kind of wind.

13. Instead, I gravitate to the sound of the word, *wind*. Sounds like *win*. As in winning the race, bodies running to the soundtrack from *Chariots of Fire* and the wind is always blowing in their hair, glorious and shiny.

Incorrectly Berthed

My nephew kicked a boy for being in his spot   knees.crossed   Exes.
Feather-faced is the window pane beaten two and half times. They say
El Niño will be pacific, but really, who wants to be a needle
among a sea of irregulars   I tease my thoughts with milk.   *This is*
the taste for today's woman. For your hands,   *for   your   lips,*
Virginia. But warm in her hands is not the boy child. Rotter's locus of
control says my efforts   reel in my wins or everything I have   is by
chance.lucky frog.clovers.what I really want to say is that I don't know
how I'll die   when I can't find my teeth   while brushing
my car.if I flower the grave and water my bed—maybe the songs are
really just songs.   Pity.the last cigarette ad aired in 1970
on The Johnny Carson Show just before midnight of the President's
ban. The last times are never known   in that moment. Tell
me again, how unmooring a boat before a storm saves it from
permanent damage?

Trajectory

It must be fulfilling knowing whom to love, that one's calling in life is to guard and growl. John Wayne had a dog named *Dog*. A clever thing able to translate *Dog!* meaning *Attack!* from *Dog!* meaning *Get your ass over here, I'm leaving.* What does it mean to name that which obeys their loved ones? They seduced a dog with food, washed the streets of Moscow out of her fur. They praised and encouraged her: *Off to college! Be a mother and have a career.* I like to imagine, they patted her head for good luck, scratched behind her ear—which she had learned to lean into. I like to imagine that when Laika had crossed that orbital finish line as the first dog in outer space, she remained ignorant of the words *hyperthermia*, *betrayal*, *dispensable*. That the evening lights and the fading metal clicks were neighborhood doors swinging open. Each threshold offering a handful of food, a gentle pat on her head. *Good girl. You're such a good dog.*

Double Entry

My mother and I wait for fortune
to fall. Our pockets plump

with college loans. In some cities,
a virgin or child is sacrificed

to quell that with fur on back and ears.
Is it better to seem compliant

or fly faster with less control?
Even water gods can tally late fees.

My mother's sacrifices are tea-stained,
like a leash-tan around my leg

skinning her past from today's last light.
I worry over holes in *zero* and *options*.

My mother and I wait for my college
degree to mean something.

She gardens peppers, tomatoes, paprika.
Edible or poisonous are aspirations.

Sometimes the body inflames
against harm, swells with pain.

The wait time, to be counted,
so long, causing dizziness

or a loss of function.

Color Interference

I thought it was a trick
of the eye, when two light waves

complement each other,
strengthening their reflection

painting rainbows in soap bubbles,
on butterfly wings, and seashells. At the

beach, a girl told her friend: "She's not
just Asian; she's white. That's why you

like her." She cautioned against pitfalls
and flaws. How falling for types is

dangerous, it usually almost
always breaks us.

It's a phenomenon, *iridescence*,
more than an optical curiosity. Its

exotic lustre helps us recognize
our same species, choose mates,

and, sometimes, evade predators.

[shoulda sd something to the young man
yelling at his wife on the next bench]

You lose
evry thought
loaned. You
ramble
untl tomorrow
is silver
with bones
untl thorns
waiver
red
redacted.

Hate Crimes Rise as Coronavirus Spreads

We strive to live in the pocket of the wave
where the energy is brightest.
On the subway at Lexington Ave./59th St.
you can pick up maximum speed
if you're held by your wrist and shoulder
uprooted from your seat.
I mean your home, I mean your country
I mean your great-grandparents' country
How you failed at making yourself smaller
in the pocket of your seat on your way to work this morning.

You resist being shot too far ahead
before you curl into your mouth,
except you find you're standing on the open face
of the wave with less energy and resistance:
nasty people should stay in fucking Asia
before punching her in the back of the head
rounded up, shipped out, denied entry
into a gas station.

You and your body, not quite out of water,
have no choice but to do a cutback—
circling back to the power source
cutting into what cuts you the deepest.
You shift your weight, driving up the face of the wave
I mean destruction, I mean humiliation, I mean
a country where a 13-year-old boy spits at your father.

You remember that the wall can close out on you
with energy to launch large rocks into the air,
damage buildings a hundred feet above its surface.
You remember that your head and chest
should face the direction where you want to go.

The Murder of Gill Jamieson: Rising Tensions Between Elite Whites and the Japanese, 1929

He had been strangled and his head chiseled in. He waited, worrying about what his mother would say now that his head was broken. He didn't know he was dying, but he feared getting in trouble. The hole in his head was more of a straight groove curving wider, falling into itself: a cul-de-sac. The roughness of space through the slanting gap felt forthright, like fingers bending through the window blinds or tonguing the space after a tooth fell out.

The moon's light and the cold night wind dipped into the shallow crevice. The whiteness and whispers embedded inside his head.

Smoke & Fire

For those "who cannot be lost or elsewhere or incomplete." -W.S. Merwin

there is no space for the enemy
between the en dash you don't know

what follows whom to hate
belief   rotates the en dash

is flatline is aperture
closing a sigh   of

scene: yesterdays numbers
camera a body dates or some

armhold one
scepter & challis to handle or toss

a line no
foothold   it's all we'd gift them   all

smoke & fire read *cursor & space*
words with diamonds the world to stay

on a band   read to stop   sorry
tears through our losses

red   means more than
fire   connections

St. Jerome Praying in the Wilderness

After the painting of the same name by Leonardo Da Vinci

you tell me the beetle will most likely

drown: i   salmon forward

stitched a carcass   or career // a miracle

verified //   to serve god

i think of all the bedsides

          i've left savory

& titian

          what   does an orchid   do

of heroic value   i once waited for a cactus

          to grow arms   like a man //   a tawny tale

we assembled a caravan   of two

golden creases   five years //   after death

who notices you halved

& peached

holding onto things // forever   like

Object Carrying

Have you heard the one where the orca
floats her dead calf for thousands of miles?
Her wings thrash briskly, vaults up pictorial
       still bonded—

Or when the aquarium worker unhinged a buoy
from a Beluga after losing her calf?

Except when I say *buoy*
             I really mean *sibilant*
             like sunset, half-opened

It reminds me of our song
when a twig breaks after day-old rain

Sometimes I feel obligated like the moon
circling a difficult subject—

Except when I say *circling*
        I mean I *never* close my eyes

             to unhook a crab's grip
             rooting under the lid—

Knowing some vessels
can take on more water than others

Cast Away

Swimming in a pool on an island
surrounded by ocean is like crying over a movie where siblings

reunite after a parent's death;
when really you're just crying over a movie where siblings

reunite after a parent's death.
Blame the soundtrack, unbottling what's urned like a child-proof

cap, a shallow wound. But in my story
I was drowning. In my story, he doesn't save or ruin me.

I swallowed panic. I drowned things
like bodies inside me, downed rain.hip first.broken in half

in a tube.no hands.the last & first
to come out of the womb, a softly stretched shirt.

I grew up & over flooded someone else's ocean
instead of diving in, lying at the bottom, lying to parents, plot-caked

tile marked. They bear the sun & shame—
increasing alertness.alarm.whirlpooling. There was no one left

to save me, save my brother. Other animals
have alternate self-protection methods.

Seconds before a wooden bowl hits the tile,
I know exactly where it will crack, like how I can spot a savior

when cold-blooded animals change colors
too swiftly—edged down, jeans spread. There are times when

I've said no to pie.to acid.to boys
who didn't know what they wanted: to camouflage themselves.

I wonder if I'm the broken part
in the wooden bowl, like a pool in the middle the ocean

holding my pieces together,
crying like crying over a movie about

I tell myself I'm not going to write another dead mom poem

Nevertheless she arrives, promptly. In a care home fisted with careless bags of food or a spam musubi. A comfort offering in reverse. I start to write about letting greyhounds be dogs again, how it's still legal to race dogs in four states. Can we even home those warehoused twenty-three hours a day? If I were the earth, even I could spin completely around. But my mom appears mid-turn, calling me by my sister's name, her sister's name, and I realize I'll never be a good mother if I'm chasing the good-daughter approval. So I ignore her, like her phone calls before she was incontinent, before being shamed by Pizza Hut's weekly delivery of chicken alfredo. I debone movies about dogs as protagonists since the endings are always the same: we canter along our dog-day, the girl in the bar, her raw bits; the boss who scratched where we didn't need scratching. I fast forward to the climactic scene, admonished in a shed in winter, waiting for someone to crack. I toggle between pause and play hoping for a different ending. My friend's in the hospital, stage four breast cancer. Her family will take care of her dog. My mom thinks this is not like the movies, *there's no dress rehearsal for life*, she tells me when I come out to her, after leaving my husband for the woman I love. Sometimes I'm tired of running and reaching. Every time I'm offered salvation, I remember I don't know how to dog. At the mouth of a large river, I dump my regrets; they solidify, compact over time into man-made cliffs, like a marriage or an emerald island, something to jump off from. I pancake my bare feet on warm rocks, bracing, waiting to try again.

Exoskeleton

Terms of endearment still fit me, no matter how relationship-worn.
Size four. Size fire horse. Orion's belt cinched part-time alarmist and
cynical. The old me and new me with each growth spiraled; tree'd
a new ring on finger. I've heeded to calls, both baritone and alto, as
either percolates me equatorial.

It's not that I mind reusing words. I love sitting my ideas in
your lap, your arms around my uncommon thoughts, lifting and
supporting my spaces. You are both rafters and birds. I gaze at your
towering western, how you bookend the spaces of my living, all my
conundrums. In all this vastness, I worry most for utilitarian words:
wild.impassable.pathless.

Do you wonder why some words hum violent and moist? exclusive.
ditch.alcoholic.undersea. out   of   reach. While some words are
bubble wrapped, laced: pallbearer.widow.molting.

And more   uncomfortable spaces.   Everyone treks
time forward and Himalayan, craggy. Better now?

words.terms.endeared ones encased.opposing ends of an em-dash. And the old you traverses the new you and sail the seven hundred stages of grief, plus one hour next and next. Every minute, every year, you icebreak.jagged.dusk and piñata. On knees, you gather pebbled moments with friends not uncomfortable in uncomfortable spaces. Then, not so suddenly, vocabulary cracks along your back between carapace and abdomen. You slowly back out in your new soft shell. still.love.vertiginous.sugar-spun.

Notes

"Fractured Planes"
   I was watching this thing that you just said hanging in the air between us is a line borrowed from Monica Youn's poem "Brownacre", *The New Yorker*, May 23, 2016 issue.
   A flower stretched over a hundred yards following itself across the desert is a line borrowed from Tonino, Leath. "The Skeleton Gets Up and Walks: Craig Childs on How the World is Always Ending." *The Sun.* June 2016. Issue 486.

"You're Trapped in School, and Your Classmates Are Turning into Zombies" references Eva de Vitray-Meyerovitch, 'Rumi and Sufism' trans. Simone Fattal Sausalito, CA: Post-Apollo Press, 1977, 1987.

"Winds are Named for the Direction They are Heading"
   In memory of Aiyana Stanley Jones.

Acknowledgements

Grateful to the hardworking editors of these publications in which this work first appeared, sometimes in different versions:

433 Magazine — "Elasticity"

Agapanthus Collective — "Le Philosophe after the painting with the same name by Giorgio de Chirico"

Anti-Heroin Chic — "Incorrectly Berthed"

Cobra Milk — "A Hundred-Pound Test Line," "Housebreak"

Crab Fat Magazine — "Hā means Breath in Hawaiian"

Feral — "Birthmark"

Fish Food Magazine — "Tues Morn" & "Irreverent Y"

Ghost Heart Lit. — "Hate Crimes Rise as Coronavirus Spreads", "to *deadhead* plants means to remove their spent flowers"

Hawaii Pacific Review — "Color Interference"

Juked — "Fractured Planes: An Empty Defense Mechanism"

Lucky Pierre Zine	"St. Jerome Praying in the Wilderness after the painting with same name..."
Mixed Mag	"I Tell Myself I'm not going to Write Another Dead Mom Poem"
MORIA	"You're Trapped in School, and Your Classmates Are Turning into Zombies" (originally "The Prompt")
Near Window Zine	
Nectar Poetry	"Trajectory"
Negative Capability Press	"Cast Away"
Phoebe	"Body Language," "Forecast," "Object Carrying"
Prometheus Dreaming	"Exploded as in Fairy Tale"
	"Reservations as Future Tense," (originally "Fruitcakes: The Strange New Fruit")
Puerto Del Sol	"Exoskeleton"
Red Tree Review	"Defect"
Riot Act	"Division"

Stone of Madness Press	"The Blue Circus after the painting of the same name by Marc Chagall"
The Daily Drunk Mag	"Salt as Preservative"
The Gambler Magazine	"On Using my Bones to Make Your Bread" & "[Shoulda sd something to the young man yelling at his wife on the next bench]"
The Maynard	"What We Do When We Run Out of Elephants"
The West Review	"Winds are Named for the Direction They are Heading"
Windows Facing Windows	"Double-Entry"

My deepest gratitude to the poets, their workshops, and institutions whose support and encouragement inspired me to push through. At Oregon State University—Cascades Creative Writing low-residency program, I'm indebted to T.C. Tolbert and Arielle Greenberg, Irene Cooper, Austin Anderson, and Laura Winberry; The (Ashberry) Home School, I'm grateful for the opportunity to be mentored by Harryette Mullen; OSU's Spring Creek Collaborative Retreat; Flight School by *Flypaper Lit*; K-Ming Chang's "Writing Family" workshop; and Jose Hernandez Diaz's "Prose Poetry" workshop. To the Po-Heads at Henry J. Kaiser High School, thank you for being the first poems I sent out into the world.

To Amy Acre and Jake Hall, an immeasurable mahalo for the care and insight provided through the editing process and support of the book tour in the U.K.

To my family, our island of mis-fit toys, Craig T. Murayama, Randi, Dylan, Travis, Haley, Shane, Kelsey, Mia, Jayden, Alden, Steve, Sarah, Jeff x2, and Squid, thank you for supporting me, always.

To you reading this book, thank you most of all.

Lightning Source UK Ltd.
Milton Keynes UK
UKHW012112170322
400106UK00006B/83